the DNA of RELATIONSHIPS

Small Group Series

Dr. Gary Smalley
Michael Smalley
with Ted Cunningham

Copyright 2005 Gary Smalley

Welcome

Welcome to the DNA of Relationships Small Group Series. We are thrilled that you have decided to invest in your relationships.

At the Smalley Relationship Center we have made it our mission to increase marital satisfaction and decrease the divorce rate. The DNA core truths are the strongest methods we know of for accomplishing that goal.

Our prayer is that the Holy Spirit will empower you as you work out these life-changing truths. Enjoy yourself. Learn. Grow. And most importantly, watch your most treasured relationships flourish.

Enjoy the ride!

Gary Smalley
Michael Smalley
Ted Cunningham

Biographies

Dr. Gary Smalley, founder and chairman of the board of the Smalley Relationship Center, is one of the country's best-known authors and speakers on family relationships. He is the author and co-author of more than forty books. Gary has also produced several popular films and videos. Gary's newest book, *The DNA of Relationships,* discovers the main hurdles to great relationships after 5 years of extensive clinical research. This new fresh look at how we are designed for relationships gives the reader methods to construct satisfying relationships with those close to them whether a spouse, children, friends, co-workers or even neighbors. After all, life is all about relationships and the rest are just details!

In his thirty-five years as a national speaker and seminar leader, Gary has spoken to more than two million people in conferences. In addition to earning a master's degree from Bethel Theological Seminary, Gary has received two honorary doctorates, one from Biola University (California) and one from Southwest Baptist University (Missouri), for his work with couples. Gary and Norma have been married for over 40 years.

Michael Smalley M.A., as an author and speaker, is changing the landscape of relationships in America with straight forward and no nonsense advice. Michael earned a Master's Degree in clinical psychology from Wheaton College in Chicago, Illinois. For the past ten years he has spoken live to millions of people around the world. He teaches with entertaining stories and illustrations to allow audiences to enjoy their time and learn through laughter. Michael has authored or coauthored relationship advice books like *Communicating with Your Teen,* the *Men's Relational Toolbox,* and *Don't Date Naked.* Michael and Amy have been married 10 years and have three children - Cole, Reagan, and David.

Ted Cunningham serves as the senior pastor of Woodland Hills Community Church in Branson, Missouri. He is a graduate of Liberty University and Dallas Theological Seminary. Ted is writing articles, devotionals and hosting the new Smalley Relationship Club with Gary Smalley. Ted and his wife Amy have been married for 8 years. They live in Branson, Missouri, and have two children - Corynn and Carson.

Table of Contents

LEADER'S NOTES . . . . **page 5**

Week 1 -   Introduction . . . . page 6

Week 2 -   Discovering Your DNA of Relationships . . . . page 9
             Dr. Gary Smalley

Week 3 -   Power of One – Taking Personal Responsibility . . . . page 17
             Michael Smalley

Week 4 -   Fear Dance – #1 Destroyer of Relationships . . . . page 24
             Dr. Gary Smalley

Week 5 -   Creating a Safe Place for Love to Flourish . . . . page 28
             Michael Smalley

Week 6 -   God's Fuel for Your Soul: Caring for Yourself . . . . page 31
             Dr. Gary Smalley

Week 7 -   Create Harmony through Communication . . . . page 36
             Michael Smalley

Week 8 -   Follow-up . . . . page 42

LEADER'S NOTES

Here are a few suggestions for implementing this guide in your small group:

1. On the first night of small group, share with them the DNA of Relationships covenant made available in Appendix B. Ask for questions and address concerns in signing the covenant.

2. As an introduction, begin each night of small group with a story from the assigned chapter.
    - Ask the small group participants in what ways they can relate to the story.
    - Give 10-15 minutes for warm-up and introduction prior to showing the video.

3. Open each week with prayer.

4. Remind group members of the need for confidentiality. Vulnerability in members will shut down if confidentiality is threatened. Remind them of the covenant they signed at the beginning of the series.

5. Here is an outline for a typical small group:
    - Warm-up, introduction, and prayer (15 minutes)
    - Video (35-45 minutes)
    - Going Deeper (30 minutes)
    - Wrap-up (5-10 minutes)

6. End by asking for goals and take-away value. Ask for ways that you, the leader, can hold them accountable.

7. Challenge the group to memorize the verse of the week. (Verse cards are provided in Appendix C)

8. Close with a prayer of commitment.

9. Be sure to remind them of the next week's session.

the DNA of RELATIONSHIPS

WEEK 1

INTRODUCTION

(SUPPORTS THE DNA OF RELATIONSHIPS BOOK- CHAPTER 1)

What if you discovered a method for restoring your most treasured relationships, renewing love for one another, and increasing your satisfaction in life? Sounds like a tall order, doesn't it? How can I do that?

This study teaches men and women alike the DNA of relationships, the pattern of their unique relationship patterns and gives simple steps for building healthy relationships.

By committing yourself to learning and practicing these principles and steps, you can not only rediscover your passion for one another but also learn how to build a fulfilling relationships.

Does it seem far-fetched that by understanding and applying a few key concepts, sour relationships can turn sweet and anger can give way to joy?

What a difference it can make when you understand and live the DNA of relationships, your unique relationship dance. As you join me in this delightful adventure of discovery, you'll experience God's love and power in fresh and exciting ways:

You'll learn about the amazing **Power of One**. You'll see how to take personal responsibility for your part in all relationships. You'll see how to become completely empowered to choose how you feel within all of your relationships. This message has completely changed our family, our staff, and our lives. We just have to send it out to the world, to churches, families, couples and singles, so that others can enjoy the same freedom and enthusiasm that we're enjoying! Can you just imagine teenagers—or anyone else for that matter—not blaming others for being unhappy? Picture teens learning how to be responsible for their own emotions.

You'll learn about **Safety**, about creating an environment that feels safe, where true intimacy can take root and bloom. You'll learn how personal differences can enhance your relationship instead of causing problems and how you can adopt an attitude of curiosity instead of judging others. And you'll discover how to effectively and positively deal with "walls" that your partner or friends may put up. Just imagine friends, couples, and kids feeling completely safe to open up and share their deepest thoughts with others who love them.

You'll learn about **Self-Care**, how God wants you to take care of yourself so that you can become a channel of His love to others. We'll show you how to make sure that your internal battery is charged, ready to connect for satisfying and fulfilling relationships. Imagine a host of people learning how to take care of themselves in ways that enable them to care for others. Can you see workplaces and churches filled with people who are not expecting others to fill them up but rather are taking care of themselves during the week and coming to work or church to enrich each other?

You'll learn about **Emotional Communication**, a powerful communication method with the strength to eliminate the main causes of divorce and the primary causes of separation between friends. You'll learn how to connect deeply with the heart of another person. We'll show you how to find the emotional "nugget" that leads to effective and fulfilling communication, enabling you to feel confident that you will be understood. And we're going to show you how to make communication easier and more efficient than you've ever experienced! Imagine feeling that others deeply understand you.

You'll learn about **Teamwork**, about adopting a no-losers policy that will help you walk in harmony and complete unity with your spouse, family members, and friends so that you never again have to worry about losing an argument. We'll show you how to identify the obstacles that make your relationships difficult, as well as how to remove those hurdles. Imagine families, neighbors and colleagues working through conflict in ways that don't damage relationships.

> Does any of this sound appealing to you?
>
> Does it sound like something you would like in your own life?
>
> Well, how could it not?

We Have a Relationship Crisis Today
What you will learn and experience in this series will have an impact far beyond your personal relationships because we are surrounded by millions of people in relationship crises. The following could be read as the headlines of a culture losing the battle for relationships:

Lifelong friendship goes sour
Teenager runs away from home
Co-workers quarrel, one leaves the company
Girlfriend and boyfriend split up
Newlyweds have first fight
Adult siblings stop talking to each other—for years
Soldier returns home from defending country and abuses his wife
Marriage of fifteen years shatters in divorce
Lonely teenager commits suicide
Pastor's marital infidelity splits church
Two students, estranged from friends and society, assassinate a dozen schoolmates and then end their own lives
Nineteen terrorists wreak havoc on a country, killing thousands of innocent people

Something has gone very wrong. We all know it. At least one of these scenarios has touched nearly every person on earth. The effects of broken relationships cut across the generations, from school children to married couples to senior citizens. And the consequences are staggering. Worse yet, the tragic stories of disrupted friendships, marriages, families, communities, and nations grow increasingly frequent.

We see that practically all the world's crises, little or large, can be reduced to one thing: the breakdown of relationships.

We believe that the message of this book can have a profound impact on our culture. Our ultimate goal is not merely to help you build great relationships but also to encourage you to take what you learn and multiply it in the lives of others around you.

Discussion Questions

- What relationships could benefit from this series?

- Are there areas of my life that seem out of control?

- Has my stress level gone up in recent years?

- Am I open to sharing my life with this small group?

- Am I open to being held accountable for growth by the group?

- Am I willing to share my struggles, challenges, and relational conflicts with them?

- How should I begin praying for the principles of this study to be unleashed in my life?

Prayer of Commitment

Father, I am ready to grow in my relationships. I want to understand and grow in my relationship with you. I need your power to make it through this series. There will probably be moments when behavior patterns of mine will be challenged. Help me to remain open to your Spirit's work in my life. These truths are too important. I so desire to grow in my relationship with you, others and myself.

MEMORY VERSE FOR THE WEEK:

I Will Pass All of My Thoughts Through the Following Grid

"Finally, brothers, whatever is true, whatever is noble, whatever is right, whatever is pure, whatever is lovely, whatever is admirable—if anything is excellent or praiseworthy—think about such things. Whatever you have learned or received or heard from me, or seen in me—put it into practice. And the God of peace will be with you."

Philippians 4:8, 9

the DNA of RELATIONSHIPS

WEEK 2

DISCOVERING YOUR DNA OF RELATIONSHIPS

(SUPPORTS THE DNA OF RELATIONSHIPS BOOK- CHAPTER 2)

CORE DNA TRUTHS FOR THIS SESSION:
- You are made for three kinds of relationships: with others, with yourself, and with God.
- It's never just about the other person.
- Put yourself in the picture.
- Get God's lens for a healthy view of your relationships.
- All three relationships must be in balance.
- Choice equals change.
- Not choosing is itself a choice.

INTRODUCTION

In this session, you are going to learn how you are wired for relationships. In fact, Dr. Gary Smalley is going to show you how to find balance in all three of life's relationships: Your relationship with God, your relationship with others and your relationship with yourself.

We don't always have the ability to choose our relationships, but we do have the ability to choose how we will respond in those relationships. Gary will also help us to control our thoughts and responses to stressful events and circumstances in our lives. If you are alive and breathing, then you need this session.

PLAY VIDEO SESSION 1 (46 minutes)

GOING DEEPER

*"To **love the Lord God** with all your heart, soul, mind and strength and the second one was like the first; **love your neighbor** in the same way that you **love yourself**."* Matthew 22:37

You are made for three fulfilling relationships.
You are designed to seek loving, fulfilling and safe relationships with God, others and yourself. Each of these

relationships is not only important, but each is intricately related to the other. Everyone wants deep, connected, safe, intimate relationships.

"God has put within you the desire to love Him and others like yourself."

Within the human brain, God has placed an area that draws us to meaningful and fulfilling relationships. Dr. Allan Schore of UCLA, neuroscientist and developmental psychologist, says that, "all humans are born to form attachments, that our brains are physically wired to develop in tandem with another's through emotional communication, even before words are spoken. Our sense of right and wrong originates largely from our biologically primed need to connect with others." Rules help, but relationships are more important. There is now scientific evidence that the genetic structure within children, on the single cell level, can be affected and changed by the type of love we receive from parents, relatives and friends.

Q. What type of relationship do you have with God, others, and yourself? Be honest with yourself and make a true evaluation. What kind of relationship with God do you desire? What kind of relationship do you want with others?

You are designed with the ability to choose.
You can't always choose your relationships, but you can choose how you will think and act in those relationships. You choose who you spend time with, your life mate, and you also choose actions that damage or repair relationships daily. You choose everyday whom you will serve, how you will follow God or how you will strengthen relationships. In "waiting or not choosing" you have made a choice.

You have three main choices:

    1. You choose each day whether you will develop fulfilling or dissatisfying relationships.

    2. You pick your priorities each day - where you will spend your time, money and energy. You can easily get out of balance with relationships. Too much time spent at work, school, shopping, etc. and you neglect loved ones.

    3. **The greatest choice of all is what you THINK about after anything happens to you daily.** It's not what happens to you that determines your emotions (anger, fear, sadness, joy, peace, loneliness, frustration, love, discouragement, etc.), it's what you think about after things happen to you that determines all of your emotions, words and actions. The greatest part of this truth is that you can no longer blame others or your circumstances for how you feel or what you say or do. Proverbs 23:7 and Galatians 6:7

    Q. Have you ever identified a pattern in your relationships where the problem is always the other person's fault? Have you ever felt helpless when the other person refuses to change?

    Q. What type of choices do you make with others? Are you willing to repair any of your relationships? Make a list of the relationships that are in need of repair.

    Q. Would you say it is time to start making some changes? List a few of the changes you would like to make.

You are designed with the capacity to control all of your own thoughts and thus, your emotions.

You are made to take responsibility for yourself. You cannot change the other person or some circumstances, but you can take responsibility for your own thoughts after something happens to you. This is the key to life. "As a man thinks in his heart, so is he" Proverbs 23:7. "Whatever a man sows in his heart, that is what he will reap" Galatians 6:7.

Thoughts- What you choose to think about and say to yourself everyday determines all of your emotions. Look around your house one day; just stare at your driveway or front yard or apartment. Everything you have started with a simple thought.

Responses- What you think after each experience, good or bad, determines your emotions in an hour or a month. It's not what happens to you that determines your fullness of life; it's how you choose to use your thoughts in response. The sooner you receive God's Spirit within you and use His power to choose to think like Jesus Christ (Let His mind be in you... Philippians 2:5), the faster you'll enjoy the fruit of the Spirit: love, joy, peace, patience, self-control, kindness, goodness, etc. For example, Gary's stress level was cut by 80% in one day by learning to give up many of his expectations and hand them to God. As soon as he took the time limits off all the remaining expectations, his stress dropped dramatically in 24 hours. His thoughts and expectations (these are thoughts too) were starting to focus on things above and not on the things of this world. Col. 3:1-17
You will find that as you start controlling what you think to be more in line with God's will for your thoughts, you will start receiving more of God's love and peace.

Six Illustrated Scripture Sections that Can Ignite Your Inner Power and Fulfillment in Life

Gary reviews these six sections at least twice per day. He testifies that the following verses have transformed his thinking and given him more power, love, fulfillment and life than at any other time in his life

1. You have the capacity of containing **unlimited** power, love, fulfillment and life when Christ's Holy Spirit lives inside of you. (Eph. 3:16– 20) His power within you is evidenced by your amount of love toward others, your ability to live His will for you, your sense of peace and fulfillment on a daily basis and your overall Christ like character. You will read later how His power grows (matures, is perfected) within you each day. With God's resurrection power living within you, you can do amazing things. Whether I'm thinking of witnessing to someone, walking a mile, talking with my mate or friend, working on a major project, I'm continually aware of this unlimited power within me. He told us, His followers, that we would be able to do greater things than He did. And His power grows within you with each trial. See #6.

2. Because of the great power within you, you can take every one of your **thoughts** (beliefs, dreams, ideas) captive to the obedience of Christ. (II Corinthians 10:5) Since all of your emotions, words and actions originate in your heart and mind, you can wake up every morning with the assurance that you have the power to control how you feel, what you say and how you act all day long.

No one is a victim. If I'm on the beach and I notice a beautiful woman with a great shape, I can think that God did a great job in designing her, but if my mind starts to wander in a lustful direction, I have unlimited power to say to my mind, NO! That thought does not line up with (Phil 4:8, 9) I say to myself, "Sorry thoughts, I will not allow lustful thinking about this person." The reason is because lustful thoughts do not match any of the **Big Eight** words given to us in Phil. 4:8, 9. Those lustful thoughts are not: true, honorable, right, pure, beautiful, adorable, excellent or worthy of praise. And if my thoughts don't match this verse, I don't allow the thought to continue. "Is this really possible?" you ask. At first, I was thinking that this new power wouldn't last and that lustful patterns would return just like they always would after a "Christian Camp experience." But this time it has lasted for years. Amazing. You have the power within you to control your thoughts.

I know some of you are questioning the reality of this truth, but trust Him, it works. Just think of the power this gives you in every area of life.

3. Why would you want to control your thoughts? Because, as you think in your heart, so are you. (Proverbs 23:7) Also, whatever thoughts you sow into your mind, you will reap the consequences. (Galatians 6:7) You become what you think! Spend a few seconds reflecting on who you are today and what you have.

This is a great truth: you become what you think. Everything about you is the result of what you have been thinking. Day dreaming is thinking, planning is thinking, imagining is thinking, doubt is thinking, reacting to circumstances is thinking and regretfully wishing things could have been different for you is thinking, guilt is thinking and on and on. After days, months and years of thinking certain thoughts like, "Oh this is bad that my father says horrible things to me, I wish I had never been born, I must be a very bad person," you soon develop a deep belief about yourself. Any continual practice of thinking negative thoughts will catch up to you in negative emotions, words or actions.

When deep negative beliefs develop within you, how do you break them?

When something "bad" happens to you, you are in control of what you think about this "bad" thing. What are your continual thoughts **after** any "bad" thing happens to you? Those thoughts determine your future emotions, words and actions. Look around where you sleep at night. Your jobs, car, trips, fun times, friends, actions and words are the result of your thoughts. Start reflecting upon your past thoughts and see if Galatians 6:7 is true in your life.

The range of emotions from joy to sadness ALL come from your thoughts. Continual thoughts in the same areas soon become beliefs. You have no one to blame for what you are today but your own thoughts. Everyday I use my mind to dream dreams about my life and future. I imagine myself on TV programs talking about what I'm doing and seeing millions of lives change as they buy my new book and then, allow me to coach them daily in my new Smalley Relationship Club.

I think about people in Africa emailing me and watching me on the internet learning this new message. I actually expect people in all countries of the world to email me and when I open my email in the morning, I expect to see notes from people every where. I bring my future dreams into my daily thoughts as if they are happening today. See the power in prayer available to you in Mark 11:22-24.

For over 40 years, this is how I've been living. Everything I dream about comes true in time, not always the exact way I dreamed it, but close enough to satisfy me. (Mark 11:22-24) Before my first book was published, I used to walk into book stores and tell my young children that I would give them each $10.00 for every one of my books that they could find. They would say, "Dad we couldn't find one." I'd say, "Well, you will someday, trust me." One year later, I got my first book contract. I never doubted because "all things are possible through Christ who strengthens us." (Phil 4:13)

I never did independently dream up ministry ideas and then expect God to fulfill them. I took months or years to wait for God's peace in every ministry dream or direction. I "let the peace of Christ within me control what I started imagining." (Colossians 3:15) I sought the wisdom of others who were godly, waited for my family to confirm the direction we should move, imagined every aspect of a ministry idea to see if it would lead to godliness in everyone's life including my children, friends, co-workers and so on. (I Timothy 4:6) I was very aware that God can do anything we keep asking Him to do. I was also told to be careful about what you dream because it will come your way eventually. In other words, I wanted what I did in the future to be what God wanted, not what I wanted.

> One of the greatest truths in life: It's not what happens to you (your past, present or future circumstances) or what people do or say to you that determine your emotions. Your emotions, words and actions come from what you think about after things happen to you!! You control all of your emotions, words and actions by what you think. Emotions, words and actions are data telling you what you have been thinking.

4. With the power of the Holy Spirit living within you, your thoughts can literally keep your mouth shut before you speak and as you control your words, you can control every other part of your body. (James 1:19, James 3:2) And even more importantly, as you are quick to listen, you can slow down your speech to conform your words to 8 standards.

Let your mind dwell on only these **8 powerful, life changing words. I call them The Big Eight**: true, honorable, right, pure, beautiful, adorable, excellent and praise worthy. (Phil 4:8, 9) Just imagine being able to control all of your thoughts leading to the control of your emotions, words and actions. You can control every part of your body!

What tremendous power over your life today and forever. No one controls how you think and thus, no one has the power to control how you feel, speak or act any longer. You are never the victim to others or circumstances.

Recently, my wife interrupted my decision to feed my two grand children dinner the day before a big party of sixty people. She cleared her throat and gave "that look" as she tried to smile. My wife had just finished cleaning the house, decorating it and had the meals all slow cooking in the house. I didn't notice the food cooking and invited my daughter, son-in-law and their children to join us for dinner. My wife's look and noises sounded controlling and belittling. I started to say something, but stopped, by His power within me. I began to think about what was really true here. It did make instant sense that having the kids over would be a big mistake and we really could make dinner over another dinner. Plus, my core fear is being controlled and belittled at the same time. As I thought inside myself, I realized that I am under God's control.

Second, I want to humble myself to others as Christ did by low listing myself in treating others as more important than me. Sounds like Phil 2:2-8, doesn't it? So, when I spoke words to my wife, I thanked her for reminding me of the party tomorrow and suggested that we all go out for dinner. Every one liked that idea. Especially my daughter Kari because I suggested that I would pay.

5. Now that you have this new power within you and you are controlling your thoughts, the words coming out of your mouth can be honorable not unwholesome. (Ephesians 4:29) Just imagine, you can control your words.

I know a couple who came very close to divorcing. He had an affair and his wife had a hard time trusting him, especially if he was late for dinner or late coming home after work. Once when he was late, she accused him of seeing "her" again. He started to defend himself and speak harsh words to her about "this never ending mistrust." But instead, he thought for a few seconds before opening his mouth and realized just how forgiving and loving she is to have stayed in the marriage. Then, when he opened his mouth, he spoke words of kindness and love by saying, "thank you for your continual love and commitment to me and your never ending forgiveness. By questioning me right now, it only proves to me how much you love me and I am so grateful to you!" When he started to react, he caught himself remembering what a great wife she is. If you'll slow down your verbal reactions and take the time to think about what is true about the person with whom you want to react, you'll be amazed with the words coming out of your mouth. That is James 1:19 in action.

6. Finally, when you experience trials and you are reminded of your weaknesses and shortcomings, you can actually start thinking exalting, boasting, honoring **thoughts** about your trials and weaknesses and start thinking about how much **more joy, power and godly character** you will soon have. (**Romans 5:3 – 5, James 1:2 – 4, II Cor. 12:9,10**)

This sixth point has changed me more than anything in the shortest time span. Just imagine, all of your trials and weaknesses give you more of His love, more godly character and His power is perfected within you with each passing "blow" in life!!! With His "unlimited power" living within you, you can start boasting about your trials even as the emotional pain of a trial is lingering inside you.

This is the great secret of moving from sadness to joy in a shorter time span. This is not easy and it does take practice, but it works like a miracle. I never know how long the pain will last when I'm in a trial, but I now know that the pain will eventually end and be replaced with joy, peace and more love. Having "exalting thoughts" in the midst of a trial seems so unnatural. It reminds me of Isaiah 55:8f, "'For my thoughts are not your (God's) thoughts, neither are your ways My ways', declares the Lord. 'For as the heavens are higher than the earth, so are My ways higher than your ways. And My thoughts than your thoughts.'"

When I wake up every morning and before I fall off to sleep at night, I let my mind go over all of the above verses and other verses I have memorized like Col. 3:1-17 (Wonderful truths). I now love thinking about my weaknesses, mistreatments, trials, insults, distresses and everything else that hurts me.

Because with each one of these painful circumstances, I get to boast in them knowing that I get more of His love, more of His character and more of His power growing within me each day. This is what is leading me to greater maturity. My trials are my blessings today and therefore, my thoughts about my trials are very positive resulting in more joy, peace and love. I now can think this way in the middle of feeling great pain from a trial. I allow the emotional pain because the pain is the result of my initial thinking immediately after a trial and old thought habits I still have regarding some trials. Plus, I'm far from being as mature as God desires and therefore, I will continue to feel emotional pain with trials, but it will get easier and it will take bigger trials to bring me down emotionally.

I actually rate each daily trial or hardship. I have bronze, silver and gold medal trials. There is one trial that I have had in recent years that is so big, the pain has lasted for months. There are days when I don't think about it, but it creeps into my mind several times each week. I am aware that my feelings of pain and emotional sickness are directly due to my own thinking that this trial is "bad" and in reality, it is a big trial and it is a bad thing that has happened. When I am reminded of it, my stomach is sick not only for me but because others are being hurt by the same trial.

The trial is a **huge promise that was made to me and it was broken in a giant way.** I was devastated. I wanted to give up life and run from everything I was doing. The pain was unbearable. But each day when the pain arrives, I rejoice, boast, exalt, and lift up this trial knowing that it is a massive gold medal trial. This trial has already given me more of God's love and character and is enlarging His power within me more than any other trial for the past twenty years. It's a "biggy" and I am very grateful that God allowed it to come my way. This trial is so big; I may not need another one for the next twenty years. I will gain so much from this one alone. I can't wait to see all of the joy, love, power and character it will eventually bring me. And I can't wait to see how God uses it in my life and ministry. The results are going to be big!

The key to what I am saying is that you can thank God in the middle of the pain hoping for His power and character gifts to come your way in the future days, weeks or months ahead. (Romans 5:3-5) And they will come. With some of my trials, I get peace in hours or days, but with other ones that are huge, it sometimes takes weeks or months. But hope never disappoints me. He is always faithful to his word that I will have peace, joy and love eventually. (Romans 5:3-5) And the deeper I go with Him through trials, the wider He seems to spread the message He has given me.

So, in the middle of this huge trial, I just keep boasting about it to Him and waiting for Him to end the pain and replace it with joy and other good things. How long it lasts depends upon me using His power to exalt the trial with enthusiasm hoping for the day I will be rid of the pain. But I want the pain to last long enough to do the full work within me. (James 1:2-6)

Like Paul, this pain could last for a lifetime, but if it does, oh how much power, love, godly character and other great things will be mine for His glory and for the good that will come to others through me. (II Cor. 12:7-10) It very well may be "the thorn in my side." (II Cor. 12:8)

TAKE GARY'S CHALLENGE FOR ONE WEEK
For the next week, take the following steps in changing your emotions.

As your thoughts change over time, your whole life changes including your emotions, words and actions. The following is a series of verses that allow us to change our emotions, our words and our actions. Christ living in us gives us power that has no limit. That power gives us unlimited love, peace and fulfillment. We can have more consistent peace, joy and love when we rest and rely on that power. Others will see God's powerful spirit within us and will ask us for the reason. Take these seven Biblical steps every morning and night.

1. Because I have God's Holy Spirit living within me, I have **unlimited power**, love and fulfillment. (Eph. 3:16-20)

2. As I relax and enjoy God's power within me, I can **control** all of my **thoughts** (II Cor. 10:5), **my tongue** and **my whole body** (James 3:2). (My own thoughts are what determine my own emotions. I no longer give others or circumstances the power to control my emotions. I blame my thoughts.) He has given me His Holy Spirit because I have **humbled** myself by admitting my need for His power (James 4:5, 6). What this means is that He has made it possible, through His power within me, to think thoughts that bring me joy and peace.

3. With this new power within me, I can now limit my thinking and run all of my thoughts through his grid of the **Big Eight** thoughts that bring God's peace, love and joy (Phil. 4:8,9).

4. Before I speak to others now, I can wait a few seconds while I **change** my thoughts to line up with Phil. 4:8, 9 and James 1:19. Are my thoughts true, valuable, righteous, pure, beautiful, adorable, excellent and worthy of praise? If not, I have the power to deny the wrong thoughts and change them to match God's thoughts in Phil. 4:8, 9.

5. Because my emotions, words and actions all come from my thoughts, my whole life is changing so that now, the **words** that come out of my mouth are not unwholesome towards others or circumstances, but words that build others up in love (Eph. 4:29, James 1:19). Because of James 1:19, I can slow down and keep my mouth shut until I can say words that build the other person up and not use words that take value from them.

6. Best of all, as "bad" things happen to me or have happened to me, I get to start thinking about **how much joy I will have** in a few minutes, hours, days or months because I am going through or have gone through a trial (James 1:2ff). This is where the most change has taken place in my life and others can see my peace and joy.

Here's an example: My carry-on case was stolen recently with very important items inside. My first thoughts were panic and remorse over the loss. After about twenty minutes of grieving, my thoughts turned to James 1:2-4. I instantly started thinking of all of the **joy** I will receive from God because this was a big loss and a big trial. I was being transformed within by my new thinking. I relaxed and became grateful knowing what was in store for me, but I still hurt emotionally for about 10 hours because of my maturity level and my initial negative thoughts.

When it was all over, I realized that I had backed up the most important things on my computer and the insurance would pay for the great loss including my wife's 40th wedding anniversary gift. Also, my words were more honoring toward others concerning my loss. I was surprised to hear words coming out of my mouth towards this loss that were words of praise toward God. This same truth is also applicable to big trials that happened in our past. As we start looking for how God has developed more of His love within us because of past trials, we can become grateful that "bad" things happened to us years ago.

7. I want my life to be a reflection of God's spirit of love and joy and He is transforming me even as my thoughts change because of His power. I never try to change my feelings because they are only reflections of what I have been thinking. It's my thoughts that I work on and my feelings just obediently follow. I now love to relax and listen to my feelings. I try to figure out what thoughts created them and then, I get to change my thoughts and wait for my feelings to catch up. With this truth, we can tear down and take captive stronghold thoughts (deep beliefs), imaginations and every kind of thought unto the obedience of Christ (2 Corinthians 10:4, 5).

For me, this is the best time of my life!

WRAP-UP

What is one goal you want to set for deepening a relationship? For example, you may consider stopping your blaming of others for how you feel about them because you know you are responsible for all of your thoughts about them.

How can your small group support you and pray for you in the meeting of this goal?

MEMORY VERSE FOR THE WEEK:

Before I Speak, I Will Wait a Few Seconds to Change My Thoughts
*My dear brothers, take note of this: Everyone should be quick to listen,
slow to speak and slow to become angry…*

James 1:19

the DNA of RELATIONSHIPS

WEEK 3

THE POWER OF ONE:
TAKING PERSONAL RESPONSIBILITY

(SUPPORTS THE DNA OF RELATIONSHIPS BOOK- CHAPTER 4)

CORE DNA TRUTHS FOR THIS SESSION:
- Your thoughts control your feelings and reactions.

- You are in charge of your buttons.

- You can stop the Fear Dance.

- Forgiveness heals relationships.

INTRODUCTION

IMPROVING YOUR RELATIONSHIPS BY CHANGING YOURSELF

In this session, Michael Smalley will help you take the finger of blame off of the other person and place it back on yourself. You will see the importance of stopping the blame game. Isn't it something how all of our problems are always somebody else's fault?

Michael will help you understand how you are your own worst enemy. This session will walk you through the benefits of taking responsibility for actions, choices and feelings. It will also point out the negative effects if we choose to continue to blame others. Personal responsibility is the first of the 5 new dance steps we are learning about.

PLAY VIDEO SESSION 2 (40 minutes)

GOING DEEPER

Circle the thoughts or words that best describe your frustrations in relationships:

- *"You don't see it do you? You're too negative and it's driving me away!"*

- *"You say you're sorry, but you keep doing the same mean things over and over. You'll never change!"*

- *"It's your fault that he talks to me like that, you're a great example!"*

- *"Forget it then. Go out with your friends, see if I care! Stay out all night, you like them better than me anyway."*

- *"I'm not talking about that any more, it's too hurtful."*

- *"I'll just leave the house if you continue talking about this. End of discussion; its over."*

- *"That subject is not open for discussion."*

Research over the past several years has consistently listed financial issues as the number one cause of divorce. But do you want to know something amazing? Financial problems never caused even a single divorce! They may provide the topic of angry discussion, but they don't *cause* anything.

Is the problem the other person's behavior (or attitude or personality)? "My wife is always belligerent. I want her to quit yelling at me." "My husband spends too much time at work."

It's never just about the other person. The problem is that most of us spend all of our time and energy talking about what the other person is doing or not doing.

Whenever you focus your attention on what the other person is doing, you take away your own power. You make yourself weak. In focusing on the other person, you try to control things you can't control. For that reason, it's an exercise in total futility, inefficiency, and ineffectiveness. Could that be why Jesus talked about "the log in our own eye" instead of always focusing on the faults of others?

Take a look at Matthew 7:1-5.

¹ Do not judge, or you too will be judged. ²For in the same way you judge others, you will be judged, and with the measure you use, it will be measured to you.
³ Why do you look at the speck of sawdust in your brother's eye and pay no attention to the plank in your own eye? ⁴How can you say to your brother, 'Let me take the speck out of your eye,' when all the time there is a plank in your own eye? ⁵You hypocrite, first take the plank out of your own eye, and then you will see clearly to remove the speck from your brother's eye.

Q. What word does Jesus use in verse 5 to describe a person who keeps the focus on someone else's faults?

Q. Looking back on some of your frustrations, can you identify a common cause? If so, what is it?

Next, take a look at James 4:11-12.

¹¹Brothers, do not slander one another. Anyone who speaks against his brother or judges him speaks against the law and judges it. When you judge the law, you are not keeping it, but sitting in judgment on it. ¹²There is only one Lawgiver and Judge, the one who is able to save and destroy. But you—who are you to judge your neighbor?

Q. Who is the only one with the right to judge?

Q. What are we doing when we judge?

We should expect judgmental statements directed toward us from the world, but our most treasured relationships should be "judgment-free" zones. In what ways do you find yourself to be the most judgmental? Is it the way your spouse drives? Is it the way your business partner interacts with clients? Is it the way your adult children discipline their children?

When in conflict do you work on the other person to break them down? To keep the fight going until they finally give into your way of thinking?

Take a look at this couple's story to discover how their conflict was resolved.

Between sessions at a marriage seminar in the Midwest, a clearly distressed couple, Dan and Celeste, approached me. I had just finished a segment on how couples should always try to find a win-win solution to their conflicts so that neither partner feels like a loser.

"We just don't see how we can possibly find a win-win to our problem," the exasperated woman said.

"Really?" I answered.

"It's impossible," Celeste insisted. "My husband has been out of work for six months, and our conflict is about where we should live."

Dan cut in and quickly explained that he had been applying for work everywhere but had found nothing. Recently an employer about three states away had offered him a job. "But my wife is not agreeing to the move," he said, irritation in his voice. "She won't let us go. She just won't do it." Both partners seemed very tired, a little angry, and extremely frustrated.

"So what do you think your problem is?" I asked.

"The problem is that my wife wants to stay here, in the town where we've lived for the last ten years, and I want to move so I can work and provide again for my family."

"Okay," I said, "so the conflict is about whether you stay or go?"

"Yes, basically," Dan agreed.

I shook my head. And then, to the great surprise of both husband and wife, I declared, "That's not actually your problem." And with that, I started teaching them about the dance that was destroying their relationship.

What's the Problem?

What I was saying to Dan and Celeste is that their "surface" problem is not the real problem. I was touching on a DNA truth: The external problem is rarely the real problem. In other words, what appears to be the problem is often not the problem.

As we move into this chapter, think about the trouble spots in your own relationships. What do you think the problem is in each of them? Try to name it. Now keep an open mind as you think about the DNA truth—that the conflict you've named may not be the core problem.

So what was Dan and Celeste's problem? In order to help them find out what it was, I kept asking them one basic question: So what? This was not a flippant question that dismissed their problem as if it were nothing important. It was a serious question: Why, in your mind, is that a problem?
I started by asking Celeste, "So what if you move to this new state? Why is that a problem?"

"Well, I wouldn't be around my family and my friends," she answered.

"So?" I responded, trying to help the woman understand the deeper issue. "Why is that a problem for you?"

"Because they're an important support group for me," she said.

"Okay," I replied, "but you have a husband who will support you. And you'll find other people. Why is it a problem that you would have to leave this particular support group?"

After a few minutes of gentle probing, this visibly distressed woman finally came out with it: "I just don't feel like I'm No. 1 in my husband's life."

"Ah," I declared. "I think we're finding out what the real problem is."

At last she found the words to articulate the real problem, and it wasn't the move. "I feel unimportant, as if I'm not a priority," she said to me, "so it scares me to move. I'm afraid I'll end up alone." Then she started crying.

As the husband silently took in all of this, I stopped and turned to him. For the next few minutes, the two of us went down a similar line of questioning. At the end, the man also started crying. "Honey," he said to his wife, "I don't feel like a man. I'm afraid that if we stay in your hometown, I will continue to feel controlled. I feel that your family controls everything about our lives."

Do you see it? The problem was not the move. The problem was that Celeste felt unimportant and that Dan did not feel as if he had control over his life.

And notice something else very important about their problem. At the heart of the matter, they both felt afraid.

What about you? Ask yourself the "So what?" question. Ask it several times. Where does it lead you? Where it leads you may be at the heart of your relationship problems.

After I helped them to identify their core fears, it became very clear that the real problem was not about the move. I also helped them to see themselves in the picture; it's never just about the other person.

So is that it? Are we done?

Hardly! It's one thing to identify the fear buttons that drive any particular conflict; it's quite another to break the rhythm of the Fear Dance. While I'm thrilled that this couple broke their stalemate about where to live, I believe they have a lot more work ahead of them. This was a great first step! But to continue down this satisfying road, they have to learn personal responsibility.

WHAT IS PERSONAL RESPONSIBILITY?

- We are responsible for our own **choices**, **feelings**, and **actions**.
- We can not **blame** anything or anyone.
- We can **point** our **fingers** at ourselves.

When conflict raises its ugly head, where do you place blame? Your spouse? Kids? Boss? Job? Church? Money? What steps could you take to accept personal responsibility in your life?

How would your co-workers describe your reactions in conflict? How about your family and friends? What words would they use? Would they say you mostly blame others for how you feel and act or would they say that you hardly ever blame others for your current feelings and actions?

It doesn't help a relationship—not in the least—to focus on all the "stuff" you think the other person needs to change. On the other hand, it's enormously useful to address what you are doing, to look at your own reactions, and to ponder your own fears and emotions. It does help when you do your own personal work about your own life.

"When my wife and I get into something," says one of my coworkers, "I have the ability to go off by myself and start thinking, *Okay. When I reacted that way, I wonder where that was coming from.*" We have found that is very productive. It's a waste of time, however, to talk about the other person's behavior or reactions.

Remember this: when your buttons get pushed, they're *yours*, and *you* are responsible for them. How much more productive it is when you can honestly say, "Wait a moment! These are *my* buttons. It's *my* job to understand where that came from, what that's about, and to control my reaction when my buttons get pushed."

Conflict is resolved much quicker when we focus on changing ourselves rather than others.

WHAT DO MOST PEOPLE USUALLY SAY?

- I want you to **fix** me.
- Life is **unfair**.
- God has **asked** too much of me this time.
- My **parents** made me what I am today.

Adulthood has nothing to do with birthdays and the passing of time. You become an adult by realizing you are not a victim of your past, your present, or your future. Instead of blaming, you substitute choice. You are responsible for your own thoughts, feelings, and actions. This is the essence of the power of one.

By nature, most of us want to blame those who upset us. We work hard to try to get them to change how they treat us. We attempt in many unhealthy ways to manipulate them and to force them to quit pushing our buttons.

But what usually happens when we take this approach? It succeeds only in pushing the other person's buttons, which in turn continues and accelerates the conflict. We wind up feeling hurt, abused, estranged, and lonely.

To take personal responsibility means that you refuse to focus on what the other person has done. Too many of us think, *If only my friend would say this* or *If only my husband would do that*, rather than thinking, *I can't change him, but I can change how I react to him.*

Personal responsibility requires you to take a hard look at your own side of the equation. You might say to yourself, "You know what? This person just pushed my button. Normally I would withdraw and run away, even though that solves nothing. But I'm not going to do that this time. This time I'm going to take responsibility for how I act, rather than trying to manipulate this person into acting toward me in a way I prefer."

Maybe you're a blamer. Frustrated with your job, you struggle through all of your relationships. You blame your problems on trivial things. Blaming others makes winning almost impossible because arguments and fighting usually result.

I encourage you to resist making "you" statements such as, "You're the one who needs to change," "You should have warned me that our marriage was in trouble," "You're not the same woman I married," and "You weren't submissive enough," as reasons for *your* behavior. These "you" statements are devastating, and they seldom improve your situation.

Using a statement such as, "You were just being too sensitive," stirs up more anger. As this happens, the blaming backfires and exposes your resistance to improve or change.

You are emphatically *not* at the mercy of those who push your buttons. They do not control how you react. You do not have to give them the power to determine what you think or what you do. You must take control of yourself and your emotions. You must learn that blaming others for your insecurities and fears is a dead end.

Q. *As you reflect on your relationships, in what areas of your life/thoughts/behaviors would you like to work on being more personally responsible?*

Q. *Are your thoughts true as recorded in Scripture about trials, gossip, view of yourself, God's love, and all other circumstances and things that happen to you?*

Q. *Is it easier to point the blaming finger at someone else rather than to look closely at yourself? Ask yourself "why"?*

Blaming others for our problems and conflicts has become a mainstay in our culture. If we're going to change, then it is going to take some new decisions.

Observe for a minute James 4:1.

What causes fights and quarrels among you? Don't they come from your desires that battle within you?

Does your conflict come from others? According to James, who is to blame for your conflict?

Read Eugene Peterson's paraphrase of Romans 12:2.

"Don't become so well-adjusted to your culture that you fit into it without even thinking. Instead, fix your attention on God. You'll be changed from the inside out. Readily recognize what he wants from you, and quickly respond to it. Unlike the culture around you, always dragging you down to its level of immaturity, God brings the best out of you, develops well-formed maturity in you." (MSG)

Q. What decisions will you make in stopping the blame game? List some problems and the people you have been blaming. Will you go to them and ask for forgiveness? Will you identify your role in the problem?

Look at the mandate Jesus gives us in Luke 17:3-4.

"If your brother sins, rebuke him, and if he repents, forgive him. ⁴If he sins against you seven times in a day, and seven times comes back to you and says, 'I repent,' forgive him."

Q. Even if you've been a blamer for years, you can start afresh and be forgiven. Who do you need to go to for forgiveness? To whom do you need to offer forgiveness?

WRAP - UP

- *How would you ask someone pushing your buttons to help you along on your maturity journey?*

- *At the start of this session you were asked to circle some words or statements that best described your frustrations in relationships. Now that your focus is on you, how do those words or statements change?*

- *How can the group hold you accountable in practicing this new dance step?*

MEMORY VERSE FOR THE WEEK:

I Will Only Use Encouraging Words
"Do not let any unwholesome talk come out of your mouths, but only what is helpful for building others up according to their needs, that it may benefit those who listen."

Ephesians 4:29

the DNA of RELATIONSHIPS

WEEK 4

FEAR DANCE:
THE NUMBER ONE DESTROYER OF RELATIONSHIPS

(SUPPORTS THE DNA OF RELATIONSHIPS BOOK- CHAPTER 3)

CORE DNA TRUTHS FOR THIS SESSION:
- The external issues that cause escalating arguments are rarely the real problem.
- You wrestle with a core fear.
- Don't expect the other person to be your solution to harmony and peace at home.

INTRODUCTION

In this session, Gary gets right to the heart of the matter. He will show you what is really driving the conflicts you experience in relationships. And the answer may surprise you.

Do people push your buttons? This session focuses on the buttons. Rather than changing the people around you, you will learn how to change your reactions and feelings when your buttons are pushed.

PLAY VIDEO SESSION 3 (39 minutes)

GOING DEEPER

Then the man and his wife heard the sound of the LORD God as he was walking in the garden in the cool of the day, and they hid from the LORD God among the trees of the garden. ⁹But the LORD God called to the man, "Where are you?"
¹⁰ He answered, "I heard you in the garden, and **I was afraid** *because I was naked, so I hid."* Genesis 3:8-10

Q. *In the above passage, can you identify man's common response to God? What's the problem? The Core problem.*

Q. *What statements directed toward you by others upsets you the most? Can you give 2 or 3 examples?*

The destructive dance that everyone engages in usually stems from fear. Every person struggles with some core fear. The two most common core fears are losing power with others or over circumstances (feeling controlled) and the threat of a relationship disconnect with others. Most women have a core fear related to disconnection (separation), which is the fear of not being heard, not being valued, losing the love of another or being alone. Most men have a core fear of helplessness (losing power), feeling controlled, fear of failure, or getting stepped on or misused.

- Most women have a core fear related to **DISCONNECTION** — they fear not being heard, not being valued, somehow losing the love of another.

- Most men have a core fear of **HELPLESSNESS** or feeling **CONTROLLED** — they fear failure or getting stepped on.

The Fear Dance.

Identifying your core fear is important because fear is the music that starts the relationship dance. When we try to stop the other person from making us feel our core fear, the other person is simply revealing what our core fear is. In reality they are giving us an opportunity to choose a better course of action that will allow us to deal with our core fear in a healthy manner.

The Steps in the Fear Dance.

In essence, the cycle begins when your feelings are **hurt** or you experience that heart, gut emotional pain. Then you **want** to stop feeling this emotional pain and want the other person to stop treating you in such a way that "causes" you to feel this pain. You **fear** they won't change, so you **react** and try to motivate them to change. In doing so, you start the same process in the other person. They hurt, want, fear and react. And the dancing begins. Remember, the issues that started the conflict are rarely the problem at all. The fear dance can start with discussions of sex, money, in-laws, disciplining children, room mate disagreements or anything. The problem is our core fears that keep the argument going and escalating.

Your Dance. Let's look closer.

- "You Hurt"- What does your hurt look like? Think of the range of emotions you feel when you are wounded.

List the issues, people or problems that you tend to blame for your stuck relationships. Describe your typical hurt in 2-3 sentences.

_____

_____

_____

- "You Want"- When hurt, you want a solution. You want to make it feel better. This is where you may think that the other person should make you feel better because you think that they caused the hurt. When you expect people, places and things to fulfill your wants, you'll be disappointed.

*Q. Do you see the other person as both the **cause** of your hurt and the **solution** to your hurt? (That is, if they change and stop " hurting" you) How do you respond when others "push your fear buttons"? What solution do you look for when hurt?*

• **"You Fear"**- You want to connect, be accepted, respected, etc. but you fear the other person will not change and treat you in ways that reduce your emotional pain. You want control but you fear you are powerless.
Take a look at the following Common Core Fears. Which ones do you identify with when someone hurts you?

Common Core Fears:
I get upset and feel fear when I feel....
1. Helpless, powerless, impotent, or controlled
2. Rejected; as if people are closing me out of their life
3. Abandoned or left behind, as in divorce
4. Disconnected from others or alone
5. Like a failure
6. Unlovable; as if no one could love me
7. Defective; as if something is wrong with me; as if I'm the problem
8. Inadequate; as if I just don't measure up to others like I should
9. Pained both emotionally and physically
10. Hypocritical or like a phony
11. Inferior; as if I'm being placed below everyone else in value (belittled)
12. Cheated, ripped off or taken advantage of
13. Invalidated; as if my words and actions are being ignored or devalued
14. Unfulfilled; as if what is happening to me will lead to a dissatisfied life
15. Humiliated; as if I have no dignity or self-respect
16. Manipulated; as if others are deceiving me
17. Isolated; as if others are planning to ignore me

• **"You React"**- People fall into patterns of reacting when their buttons are pushed. Most people use unhealthy reactions to deal with fear. Most of us try different ways to change the other person's words and actions so that we will feel better. As a result, our relationships are sabotaged. It's how you choose to react when your fear button is pushed that determines harmony. (use the beginning story here to illustrate how they both reacted)

Break the rhythm of the Fear Dance.
Once you identify your core fear, the solution often suggests itself. In most cases, all it takes is a true understanding of the real underlying problem… your own fears. The best solutions are realizing that your fear is yours and it is solved by turning to God and working with Him alone. You can use books, counselors and friends, but the solution does not involve changing the other party who "causes your pain." No one or nothing "causes" your fears. You have them inside of you and they are yours alone.

The CORE FEAR SOLUTION

1. Identify your core fear or fears. (Go to Appendix A to take the Core Fear test.)

_____
_____

2. Accept your core fears as your own and stop trying to keep others from pushing your "fear buttons."

3. Move your blaming finger in towards yourself.

4. Thank God that you see your own fears and seek Him alone to work with you on your fears.

5. Mature or complete love will drive your fears from you (1 John 4:18).

Here's an example: Gary's wife did not want to have the grandkids over for dinner one evening because she had just finished decorating the house for a big party the next day. Gary reacted inside because he was feeling controlled. His thinking went something like this. "Hey, whose house is this anyway? I have just a much right to have someone over as she does." He felt controlled. He instantly used James 1:19, Be quick to listen, slow to speak and therefore, slow to anger. He listened to his own thinking and realized that to be really honest and truthful, his wife is a wonderful person and he wouldn't want the "little tornadoes" going through his house either tonight. He'd have to clean the whole place again. Then he realized he was under God's **control** and she was reminding him of that truth. Secondly, he wants to be humble - low listing himself with others like Christ was (Phil 2 5:8). The first words out of his mouth directed toward his wife were, "Thank you honey, why don't we go out to dinner tonight?" James 3:2 "If a man can control his tongue, he can control every part of his body."

WRAP - UP

Q. How affective have you been in the past at changing others?
   Good success_____ No success _____

Q. In your own words, but from the other person's perspective, how would they say you react or cope after having your own cores fears pushed?

Q. What reactions do you want to work on throughout this study? What should you do immediately after your buttons are pushed? Use a current situation at work, home or play.

Q. How do you use your self talk or thoughts to apply Phil 4:8, 9? Use only these eight thoughts when reacting to your core fears being pushed.

MEMORY VERSE FOR THE WEEK:

I Will Thank God in Advance for JOY to Come From this Trial

"Consider it pure joy, my brothers, whenever you face trials of many kinds, because you know that the testing of your faith develops perseverance. Perseverance must finish its work so that you may be mature and complete, not lacking anything."
                                                                                                                                James 1:2-4

the DNA of RELATIONSHIPS

WEEK 5

CREATING A SAFE PLACE FOR LOVE TO FLOURISH

(SUPPORTS THE DNA OF RELATIONSHIPS BOOK- CHAPTER 5)

CORE DNA TRUTH FOR THIS SESSION:
• See others as God sees them.

INTRODUCTION

In this session, Michael will help you develop a strategy for safety in your relationships. He will help you identify the walls others build to protect themselves from you. Then he will guide you through the process of restoring those relationships.

PLAY VIDEO SESSION 4 (41 minutes)

GOING DEEPER
God has placed within us a human DNA system to relate. If you want great relationships of deep connection and intimacy, you need to create safety. You'll never have the relationships of your dreams until both you and the other person feel safe to open up with each other. When you open up to someone you feel safe with, **intimacy just happens naturally**. The safer both parties feel in the presence of each other (friends or loved ones), the easier it is to open up and share your most intimate heart. You'll naturally open up and share your feelings, needs, thoughts, and beliefs when you feel safe.

Four Ways to Create Safety:

1. Learn to place **high value** on everything about the other person. As you honor the other person's uniqueness and differences, you create a safe place for your relationship to grow. Decide to highly value others.

If you want to create a safe environment that encourages healthy relationships to grow, then start by honoring those around you. Just imagine yourself giving a standing ovation like you would for someone on a stage finishing an outstanding concert, dropping your jaw in awe because you are startled by the overwhelming beauty of someone's soul. The actions are limitless to express value to those we love.

Another practical way to recognize the value (honor) in another person—and to create the safety you need in your relationship—is to keep a list of all of the good qualities of that person. I keep several such lists in what I call my Honor Journal. In it I have several pages of things I find valuable about my wife, children, and grandchildren. Sometimes when I feel frustrated with one of them, I read the Honor list rather than read them the riot act. It goes a long way in building safety.

When you have safety, you have open lines for communicating. Who wouldn't want to be open after being shown honor?

Read the following passages and identify 3 reasons why we should HONOR others.

"So God created man in his own image, in the image of God he created him; male and female he created them." Genesis 1:27 (NIV)

"I praise you because I am fearfully and wonderfully made; your works are wonderful, I know that full well. [15] My frame was not hidden from you when I was made in the secret place. When I was woven together in the depths of the earth, [16] your eyes saw my unformed body. All the days ordained for me were written in your book before one of them came to be." Psalm 139:14-16 (NIV)

Q. What are some ways you can express honor to your friends and family? What words can you use?

2. Be continually **fascinated and curious** about the unique differences in others, especially in your partner, friends, and coworkers. Never judge or criticize others for being different from you or what is "normal" to you. Praise and encourage the continual expressions of differences with others. Let others know that you will never be better than they are, but your thinking may be different from them at times. Always remember that the thinking and opinions of others are just as important as your own. Staying open to discovering new things about others will help us to understand that "normal" is different for everyone. One lifetime is never long enough to completely understand the uniqueness of others.

Read the following passage, then in your own words describe the approach we should take in the Body of Christ when it comes to valuing differences.

"Each of us is a part of the one Body of Christ... The eye can never say to the hand, 'I don't need you.' The head cannot say to the feet, 'I don't need you.' And some of the parts that seem weakest and least important are really the most necessary! ... So God put the body together in such a way that extra honor and care are given to those parts that might otherwise seem less important."
1 Corinthians 12; 13, 21-22, 24b (LB)

When two people are in conflict, they often point to their differences as the problem.

If a relationship is to feel like a safe place, it must make room for *all* of both people.

3. Rebuild **trust** every day. Commit yourself to being trustworthy. Trustworthiness exists when a person recognizes and respects the incredible worth and value of another person and remembers that they are vulnerable and can be hurt. When you take this attitude, you'll always remember and be open to repairing the damage you do. When you stop criticizing, judging, condemning and blaming others, you begin to build **trust** little by little. But every time you violate trust, start over again and again and again until you have enough power from the Holy Spirit to control your tongue and end your negative words toward others.

List some words or statements that have been used against you to bring you harm or damage.

___

For the people who used the damaging words, what would you say to them if they were sitting right here, right now?

4. Learn how to **honor the "armor" others have placed upon themselves for protection against you.** Trying to tear off their armor won't work. People place armor on when they don't feel safe with you. You need to earn it off. People who wear armor feel threatened by you or others. You can become trustworthy through consistent words and actions. The less you blame, judge, criticize, condemn, or reject others, the safer they will feel in your presence. The more you allow them to be themselves, where they feel safe to share anything with you without fear of your negative reactions, the deeper your relationship will develop.

Read the following passage and list 2 reasons why we make bad judges.

"Do not judge, or you too will be judged. ²For in the same way you judge others, you will be judged, and with the measure you use, it will be measured to you." ³"Why do you look at the speck of sawdust in your brother's eye and pay no attention to the plank in your own eye? ⁴How can you say to your brother, 'Let me take the speck out of your eye,' when all the time there is a plank in your own eye? ⁵You hypocrite, first take the plank out of your own eye, and then you will see clearly to remove the speck from your brother's eye."
Matthew 7:1-5 (NIV)

None of us likes having a relational wall. It keeps us from feeling close to the other person. We want to destroy that wall, to break down that wall.

Before you head toward the wall with a sledgehammer, think about why that wall got erected in the first place. Walls are *always* built by people who feel threatened. Behind every wall we find a person who feels unsafe. That person doesn't want to stay closed and defended, but because the environment feels unsafe, he or she builds the wall for protection and self-preservation.

WRAP - UP

Q. Would you say that you are perceptive in identifying walls others have built in protecting themselves from you? If so, outline the steps you take in attempting to tear down the wall.

Q. What relationships do you not feel safe in right now? Have you created any unsafe environments?

Q. What steps will you take towards creating more safety in your relationships?

MEMORY VERSE FOR THE WEEK:

I Have Unlimited Power Through the Spirit of God
"I pray that out of his glorious riches he may strengthen you with power through his Spirit in your inner being..."
Ephesians 3:16

the DNA of RELATIONSHIPS

WEEK 6

GOD'S FUEL FOR YOUR SOUL:
CARING FOR YOURSELF

(SUPPORTS THE DNA OF RELATIONSHIPS BOOK- CHAPTER 6)

CORE DNA TRUTHS FOR THIS SESSION:
- Self-care is essential to all relationships. If you don't take care of yourself, you will have less and less to give to a relationship.

- When we take care of our whole selves we set ourselves up for healthy relationships.

- Your emotions inform you about what you are and have been thinking.

- Identify your emotions, and evaluate whether or not they have come from true thoughts.

- Taking good care of yourself is one of the best things you can do for your family, friends, and coworkers, but balance is the key.

INTRODUCTION

In this session, Gary teaches us how to honor ourselves so that we are able to love God and others better. If you are drained emotionally, physically, relationally or spiritually, then this session is for you.

We spend ample amounts of time caring for others, performing our tasks at work, raising a family, and the list goes on and on. How do we recharge our batteries? This session will walk us through the importance of taking care of ourselves and give us some ways in which we can refuel.

PLAY VIDEO SESSION 5 (39 minutes)

GOING DEEPER
Self Care and the Great Commandment.
"You must love the Lord your God with all your heart, soul, mind, and strength. And love your neighbor in the same way that you love yourself." When you love God with every part of your being, he fills you up to overflowing with His amazing power, love and fulfillment that can grow within you to unlimited levels. Out of that overflow, you can give to others. (Ephesians 3: 14 – 20)

Self Care is about balance. It's love for God, others and ourselves. He is your main source of power through His spirit within you. Our relationships with others stem from our ability to take care of ourselves. **All three must be**

31

in balance everyday. Another way of stating this truth is to "love others in the same way that you want them to love you." Only you know what you need to be truly loved. When you know what it feels like to be loved by God and others, then, you know better how to love others.

Self-care is essential to all relationships. If you don't take care of yourself, you will have a decreasing amount of love to give to your relationships with others.

List and discuss for a few moments the many ways others could love you:

On a scale of 1-10, how charged are your batteries:

• *Spiritually* _____

• *Mentally* _____

• *Emotionally* _____

• *Physically* _____

• *Relationally* _____

Q. For any battery lower than a 10, what can you do to "recharge?"

_____
_____

You are given the charge by Christ to love and care for yourself. Don't get caught in the trap of expecting others to take care of you. You learned naturally to depend upon your parents when you were young and now, as an adult why is it natural to think that our boss, mate, kids, neighbors, etc should be motivated to take care of us?

Consider how you alone will take care of the following five areas:

• **Spiritually.** Mankind seems to need a daily reminder of God's ways in order to live His words. He empowers mankind and when they finally learn His word, they have the power to live it. We at SRC have found these very special verses help us live a victorious abundant life. I go through these verses every morning and evening: Eph. 3:16-20, I Cor. 10:5, Prov. 23:7, Gal. 6:7, Phil. 4:8,9, James 1:19, James 3:2, Eph. 4:29, Romans 5:3-5 and II Cor. 12:9,10. There are many others like Col. 3:1-17 that summarize the New Testament and many Old Testament verses you can add.

• **Mentally.** You become what you think. No one else controls your thoughts unless you give them the power over you. Your words reflect your heart. For out of a man's heart are the issues of life. Guard your heart! Control all of your thoughts (1Cor. 10:5) And only think on these Big Eight words: Phil 4:8, 9

• **Emotionally.** I control my emotions by what I think day in and day out. Allow all of your emotions to surface and accept them as yours. Don't judge your emotions because they are just data telling you what you have been thinking. Use your emotions to tell you what you need to do with His power within you. If you are upset at someone, let those emotions lead you to II Corinthians.12:9, 10 and start honoring the person and situation that upset you because you are becoming more powerful within by each trial. Your love, character and power grows within you with each trial.

• **Physically.** What do I need physically? Food, water, supplements, exercise. List all of the things we need physically to function day in and day out.

- **Relationally.** Do I create safety for others? Do I practice James 1:19 and do I have someone holding me accountable? How is my support group helping me stay accountable to keep my relationships loving?

Now see how you can do the same for others that you do for yourself. How do you teach them to take care of themselves in each of the five areas?

I know that this may sound unusual to you, but good self-care is critical for maintaining balance in life.

Picture yourself as a large battery. Pretend you have two terminals on the top of your head and several sockets on your sides, where people can plug in to you for their own needs. Your kids plug into a socket. Your spouse, co-workers, friends and family all have a socket. If you get too busy caring for others, you soon become a dead battery, of no use to anyone. Good self-care ensures that your power levels stay high, making it possible for you to continue to bless others.

Many people react strongly (at first) against the idea that in order to enjoy healthy relationships, they first have to keep themselves healthy.

Take a look at your battery today.

Q. Is your emotional battery drained? How about your relational battery or your physical battery? What are your emotions telling you about your pace of life at this moment?

_____
_____
_____
_____
_____

Take time to focus on your needs for a moment. Refuel by stopping by the gym after work, or riding a bike, or getting elbow deep in your favorite hobby. When you are refueled, you will be in better shape to care for the needs of others.

Q. Is your relationship with yourself healthy? Do you value yourself as God does? Write down three ways in which you can choose to honor God by honoring yourself.

_____
_____
_____
_____

- **We tend to plug into people, animals and other things.**
We are designed to relate, so it's only natural for us to expect that people, animals and other things will "fill" us up to satisfaction in life. And then, some fear that others will reject us and we'll lose the opportunity to be filled because we are not good, tall or pretty enough.

- **We tend to plug into things.**
Earning money is the number one thing people seek to fill their tank. Money brings all the things that people think will fill them with living water like cars, food, stimulants, travel, etc. These things can actually drain us and contribute to the negative emotions we wish we could lose. Whenever we take our eyes off of God alone, we have expectations on His creation. It's okay to have all of these earthly things, as long as they are all overflow and not our main sources of expectation. Christ will fill us up to all the fullness of God. That's really full!

Three components of good Self Care.

1. **Receiving**-God's Holy Spirit has unlimited potential. Remind yourself daily that you have Him within you right now. Use prayer, His word and spiritual friends to remind you.

Imagine that you have a living growing circle of love, character and power within your heart. Your level of maturity reflects the size of your inner circle. The more mature you are, the larger the circle. If you are upset by others often, then your circle is small, but the more power, love and character that Christ develops within you through His spirit, the less you will fear (anger, frustration, hurt). Mature love casts out all fear. (I John 4:19)

Q. What enlarges your circle more than almost anything in life?

Every time you experience pain from trials, your inner circle grows by the power of His Spirit. (Rom 5:3-5)

You must open your heart to God and others in order to receive what you need. God's spirit fills you up with unlimited power, love and fulfillment. (Ephesians 3:16-20)

You must learn to attend to your own legitimate needs and desires. Remember, your feelings provide information essential for effective self care.

Great self care is cooperating with God by thanking Him for your painful experiences **while** you feel the emotional pain. His word says to boast, exalt, honor, and lift up the trial while you're in pain so that He can do His work within you. We are what we think. When thinking how special you are because of trials (II Cor. 12:9-11), you can know that He is enlarging your inner circle of love, power and character as long as the pain endures. Embrace your pain and feel the **depths** of it. Don't deny it or minimize it. Let it do its work. (James 1:2-5)

2. **Attending**-Only you know what you really need. No one else can know what you feel and need. It's impossible. But you can make a list of your main needs and start thinking about how you will start meeting each of those needs. If you have a need outside of your own power, ask the eternal God to fill it.

3. **Giving**- Responding to the needs and desires of others. There is no way that you can take care of yourself without truly giving and serving others. If you are not giving, if you are focused only on receiving and getting full, then you are working against your own best interests.

Q. Do you take enough time out for yourself? If not, list 2 or 3 activities you can cut out to free up some time. What roadblocks might you encounter in freeing up this time? How will you handle them?

Is Self Care selfish?
Good self care is a godly thing. Jesus practiced self care. People often avoid self care because they think that it is selfish. But the opposite is true. The fuller you are, the more you have to give. The more you have to give, the more you are able to serve others. Think of the airlines and how they tell you to put the oxygen mask on yourself first and then on any children traveling with you. Good self care blesses God. Taking good care of yourself is one of the best things you can do for your family, friends, and co-workers.

Read Luke 2:52 and identify the 4 ways in which Jesus grew.

_____

_____

_____

_____

Q. Why does loving and taking care of ourselves sound selfish?

Q. What words would you use to describe your physical health right now? (i.e. tired, exhausted, chipper)

WRAP - UP

In 2-3 sentences, write one goal you have to "recharge" your batteries.
_____
_____

Q. Also, how can the group hold you accountable to this goal?
_____
_____

MEMORY VERSE FOR THE WEEK:

I Can Control All of My Thoughts
"We demolish arguments and every pretension that sets itself up against the knowledge of God, and we take captive every thought to make it obedient to Christ."

II Corinthians 10:5

the DNA of RELATIONSHIPS

WEEK 7

CREATE HARMONY THROUGH COMMUNICATION

(SUPPORTS THE DNA OF RELATIONSHIPS BOOK- CHAPTER 7-8)

CORE DNA TRUTHS FOR THIS SESSION:
- The real message is often the emotion beneath the words.
- Effective communication is a dynamic process of discovery that maintains energy in the relationship.
- Effective communication takes work.
- Communication is understanding, not determining who's right.
- Winning is finding a solution both people feel good about.
- In healthy relationships, everyone wins.

INTRODUCTION
In this session, Michael wraps up the DNA principles by teaching you teamwork and communication. How often do you feel misunderstood? How often do you feel as though your words aren't "getting through?"

Michael will give us a proven strategy for listening, understanding and validating the words of others. We'll learn that the way we listen speaks volumes to people on how important they are to us.

PLAY VIDEO SESSION 6 (36 minutes)

GOING DEEPER
*"My dear brothers, take note of this: Everyone should be quick to listen, **slow** to **speak** and **slow** to become angry..."* James 1:19

"Don't push your way to the front; don't sweet-talk your way to the top. Put yourself aside, and help others get ahead. ⁴Don't be obsessed with getting your own advantage. Forget yourselves long enough to lend a helping hand." Philippians 2:3-4 (MSG)

"Live your life in unity with others because this it is a sign of destruction to the enemy." Phil 1:28

The way you stay in harmony with your mate, children and friends is to use:

LUV Talk... The Three Roads leading to Team Spirit and Harmony

L Listen   U Understand   V Validate

1. Listen:
Listen carefully. The most important first step in remaining in harmony with others and developing a great relationship is to understand their feelings, needs, opinions, concerns and ideas. Understanding is the key to a loving relationship. When others see you trying to figure them out before you try meeting their needs, they feel safer with you and tend to respond with the same kind of love for you. When you are in disharmony with others, before starting to think about any resolutions to your disagreements or conflicts, you must have understanding of each others' needs and feelings. By listening, it does not mean we agree with the other person's ideas or thinking. You can not come to harmony unless you fully understand the other person(s). Keep listening in each area (feelings, needs, opinions, etc.) until the other person(s) believes that you understand them completely. Ask the simple question, "Do you believe I understand you enough to find a solution?" How simple is that?

Listen beyond the words to the feelings. (Ch. 7 in the DNA of Relationships Book)

Somewhere along the way, we have come to believe that real communication occurs when we understand another person's *words*. True communication usually does not occur until each person understands the *feelings* that underlie the spoken words of the other.

Suppose a wife says, "I really don't think our kids should go to public schools. I think we should home school them."

Consider carefully those two sentences. The wife used no "feeling" words but all "thinking" words. So if her husband replies, "So what you're saying is that you don't think our kids should go to public schools," he's completely missed the point. He has accurately reflected to her the words she just spoke, but he remains completely in the dark about her real concern.

The key to effective communication is listening for the feelings behind each word. What if he said, "Are you saying that you feel really concerned about our kids?" When he finds out the concerns, presto! This time, he's "got it." He's tapped into her real concern—her fear for their kids. It may take a few questions before someone will uncover their own feelings. But the simplest question is, "What are all your feelings about this issue?"

People generally feel more understood, cared for, and connected when the communication focuses on their emotions and feelings rather than merely on their words or thoughts.

Q. When listening, do you find yourself asking questions to gain deeper insight? Or is your focus on you, thinking about the next point you can make?

Describe your typical body language when you're in a conversation that you want to get out of.

Describe your body language when you're enjoying the conversation.

Q. What steps can you take in listening with your whole body in every conversation?

---

2. Understand:
Understanding comes much quicker in the atmosphere of safety. You'll see everyone relaxing and calming down more when safety is present. Avoid: Who's right or wrong, who's to blame, or what happened. No judging, criticism, or belittling. Repeat back whatever the other person(s) is saying. Listen intently to feelings, needs and requests. When others hear us repeating back to them what they are saying, it increases the sense of safety and value. Care by remaining curious and fascinated. Find out what the feelings are behind their words and actions.

The real message is often the emotion behind the words. When you listen with your heart and listen for the heart of the other person, you show that you care.

"Oh, honestly! You just don't understand me! How could we be right for each other if you don't 'get' me?"

"But I asked you yesterday where you wanted to eat. You said you didn't care!"

"*Please*! You shouldn't have to ask. You should just know. I can't be with someone who seems unable to catch perfectly obvious hints. Good-bye, Chuck."

Have you ever overheard a conversation anything like this? Maybe you've been involved in one, either on the giving or receiving end. It reflects a very common reason why many people fail at healthy, positive relationships. They fail because they believe that effective communication between people in a relationship should be simple. Easy. Effortless.

It's not! Actually, it is quite complex. And it takes a *lot* of hard work. But, trust me; it is worth every second of effort!!

Many of us get really frustrated and angry with each other, as if the other person intentionally did something stupid or purposefully failed to "get it."

If we forget that effective communication is a complex process that takes a great deal of work, we can easily find ourselves getting angry with the other person and wondering how he or she can be so dense.

Q. When we find ourselves disagreeing with someone, what steps can we take to become better listeners?
_____
_____

Try saying statements like, "Let me see if I'm hearing you right" or "So what I hear you saying is…" or "What do you feel about the issue?"

Q. When someone is sharing with you, how do you respond to let them know you're getting what they're saying?
_____
_____

What relationships in your life need greater understanding instead of more problem solving attempts?
_____
_____

A lot of men and women feel frustrated when their spouses seem to go on and on. They don't understand that the reason they may go on and on is that they don't feel *emotionally* understood. If these individuals took the time to actually uncover the emotional concerns, the conversation would move on and they wouldn't have to hear the same thing a dozen times, from six different angles.

"All I have to do is help them see that I truly understand their feelings?" they ask, amazed and delighted.

Yep. That's it. Sounds great, doesn't it?

If the people in your life—whether your mate, your dating partner, your children, your friend, or your colleague—repeats the same thing over and over, I can almost guarantee that they do not believe you understand their heart. You could say at that point, "I noticed that you are repeating yourself, and that causes me to question whether you believe I understand you. Am I missing something? Do I understand your feelings?"

It is amazing what happens when a woman feels deeply understood emotionally. She will be much more inclined to stop talking about the issue, for she no longer has any reason to keep going.

3. Validate:
Validate feelings and needs through fascination and curiosity. Suspend judgment and value the differences between the two of you. When we validate the differences rather than make them the focus of our conflict, we create safety. Ask questions like, "What would you need to feel valued by me with your feelings, needs, opinions, etc.? Do you believe I understand you?"

Q. When you find yourself in an argument, what is your goal? Is your goal to win, or be right? Or is your goal unity and harmony?
_____
_____

Q. Describe your emotions when you feel as though you have lost an argument?
_____
_____

Now on to solutions.
Resolve disagreements only after understanding each others feelings and needs through the above mentioned strategy. Think of solution ideas to help form a resolution. Share as many ideas as come to your mind with each other. The more, the better; even wild ideas. From any idea can come the solution you both like. Pray together. God does have an opinion; wouldn't His answer be the best? Agree to be team members not opponents. Settle on one idea that you both love.

Picture yourself in a rowboat, gliding down the river with your friend, coworker or spouse. Suddenly an argument erupts. You see a shotgun resting in the bottom of the boat, and to make your point, you seize the gun and start blowing holes in the bottom of your little vessel.

You might get your point across—but what happens to the boat? It sinks. And who's in the boat? Your partner . . . and you. What a fine time you'll have, celebrating your "victory" all the way to the bottom of the river!

Remember this: in any kind of significant relationship, you can't win unless the other person also wins. So in your own best interest, you have to make sure that he or she wins. For exactly the same reason, the other person has to make sure that you win. The only alternative is that you both lose.

When you choose to enter into a significant relationship with another person, you're also choosing to become a member of a team. All relationships involve choice. You can choose whether that team is going to succeed or fail. You decide whether it brings you pain or delight. It's your choice.

Q. Would you say that you work hard to see the issue from both sides?
_____

We recommend a no-losers policy? Once you establish one, things start changing pretty quickly, often dramatically. Your family and friends need to know that you are on their team. They need to know that you care about their feelings and thoughts. Such a commitment goes a long way toward creating the kind of relationships that yield joy and satisfaction rather than grief and frustration.

Imagine what would happen if your body tried to function according to the rules of a win-lose system. Suppose your heart and your kidneys got into a heated debate about which one most needed a steady blood supply, winner takes all.

"Hey, I pump blood through the whole body," declares the heart. "Without me, every organ dies—including you!"

"That may be," retort the kidneys, "but if the blood doesn't go through me, all you accomplish with your incessant pumping is to poison the entire system. And then guess who dies?"

A ridiculous argument? Of course it is. Does it really matter who "wins" the debate? Because both the heart and the kidneys live as part of a single body, what affects one affects them both. The heart cannot "win" at the expense of the kidneys any more than the kidneys can "win" at the expense of the heart. They *have* to find a win-win solution because a win-lose solution is nothing but a loss.

In a marriage relationship, there is no such thing as a win-lose solution. There is either win-win or lose-lose. No other options exist. Why? Because both of you are on the same team! Team spirit is what drives the enemy away and is strength and energy to your harmonious relationships. (Phil. 1:28)

When it comes to conflict, we need a different definition of winning. If you make winning about getting your own way—in any way, shape, or form—you're headed for the relationship rocks.

Many of us resist at this point because we really do think we know what's best in any given conflict. We usually have a fairly high opinion of our own perception of a sticky situation. Be open to the possibility that even though a particular course of action seems right to you, it really may not be the best alternative. And it certainly isn't the only one. Therefore, don't lock yourself into a single view (yours). Don't insist on your path and no other. Sure, you want to win. I do, too. But maybe winning isn't about getting your own way.

Remember, you're part of a team, whether it is your family or company. A winning solution goes beyond a plan of attack that seems merely acceptable or tolerable to you both. That's compromise, and compromises rarely make anyone feel good. Therefore, you have to redefine winning as *finding and implementing a solution that both people can feel good about.*

WRAP - UP

Q. Name the person you want to work with on LUV talk. What will they need to see and hear in you to know that you are listening, understanding, valuing and resolving?

_____

_____

Q. If that person is in the small group tonight, take a few minutes and practice this in front of the group. Be open to their feedback.

_____

_____

MEMORY VERSE FOR THE WEEK:

I Can Control My Tongue and Actions
"We all stumble in many ways. If anyone is never at fault in what he says, he is a perfect man, able to keep his whole body in check."

James 3:2

the DNA of RELATIONSHIPS

WEEK 8

LET'S START THE REVOLUTION

(SUPPORTS THE DNA OF RELATIONSHIPS BOOK- CHAPTER 9-10)

INTRODUCTION

Now that you've studied all of the principles, what are you going to do with them? Do you have a plan?

This session is designed for you and your small group to share some of the lessons learned and breakthroughs you may have experienced over the past several weeks.

Q. What lessons have you learned over the past several weeks? Jot down a few of those lessons under each one of the DNA principles:

- CORE FEARS
  _____
  _____

- PERSONAL RESPONSIBILITY
  _____
  _____

- SAFETY
  _____
  _____

- SELF- CARE
  _____
  _____

- EMOTIONAL COMMUNICATION
  _____
  _____

- TEAMWORK
  _____
  _____

GOING DEEPER

I want to extend a challenge. Get "life-on-life" with others, and help those outside of your closest circle to enjoy the benefits of strong, healthy relationships. The need of the hour cries out for you to do what you can to help multiply healthy, satisfied, revitalized relationships among the people all around you. Together we can lock arms and work toward change. We've done it before in our country's history.

A Revolution in the Making

"We have it in our power to begin the world anew," wrote Thomas Paine in his 1776 instant best seller, Common Sense, a potent little book that rallied fellow patriots and fired them with resolve to change their world. His inspiring words moved the people of the American colonies to organize, band together, and fight for their freedom.

Today we need another revolution—a relationship revolution. We need a revolution to free us from the chains of relationship discord, misery, and collapse.

I believe the American Revolutionary War provides several strategies that will help us in the relationship revolution. Several historians believe the Revolutionary War succeeded for at least three reasons:

1. The average person understood what was happening and where events appeared to be leading.

2. The people learned how to get their leaders to address their growing problems with England and to nurture a grassroots response.

3. The people took decisive action.

If we are to respond effectively at this historical crossroads to the relationship crisis we face—if we are to succeed in bringing about a relationship revolution—then we must do as America's first patriots did.

1. We must open our eyes to the relationship crisis. If we are to succeed in bringing about a relationship revolution, we must also recognize what is happening to relationships all around us and realize where we will end up if we do not take steps to prevent the disaster. Do you see what is happening all around you? Can you envision where these appalling trends will take us if we do nothing?

2. We must connect with leaders and nurture a grassroots response. In an age when women had no role in combat, Deborah Samson disguised herself as a young man and presented herself as a willing volunteer for the American Revolutionary army. She enlisted as Robert Shirtliffe and went where the action was, serving for the whole term of the Revolutionary War. She offered her services, giving whatever she could to the cause. Why did she do it? She was afraid of what would happen if she did nothing. She allied herself with a grassroots effort, knowing that if people worked together, they would succeed.

If we are to successfully pull off a relationship revolution, we must connect with our leaders, the opinion makers, as well as the movers and shakers to craft a plan of action, understanding that lasting change must happen from the bottom up. And that means you and me.

3. We must take action. The American Revolution lasted more than six bloody years and cost the lives of thousands of people on both sides of the conflict. It wasn't quick, and it wasn't easy—but history reveals what an enormous and vital role it played (and plays still) on the world's stage. The patriots who dreamed of freedom did more than talk; they took action. They did what they needed to do to make their dream into a reality.

So must we.

A FINAL NOTE

It is time to take action. We must not merely talk about a relationship revolution; we must act in decisive ways to bring one about.

We can hold meetings. We can write letters. We can hold small home groups in which neighbors and friends can come together to begin the change. We can talk with our pastors and other church leaders about igniting a relationship revolution in our community. We can teach a class focusing on relationships, or we can recruit participants for such a class.

It's time to get busy. Will you answer the call? What will you do?

We have reached a watershed moment in this country when what we decide to do now about the national relationship crisis will determine for generations to come the plight of America. Will we stand by and do nothing? Or will we take the necessary steps not only to strengthen and energize our own relationships but also to help others find the satisfaction and fulfillment they also crave from their relationships?

MEMORY VERSE FOR THE WEEK:

I Humble Myself by Admitting My Need for His Power

Or do you think Scripture says without reason that the spirit he caused to live in us envies intensely? But he gives us more grace. That is why Scripture says: "God opposes the proud but gives grace to the humble."

James 4: 5, 6

More help from the Smalleys:
Smalley Relationship Club. Gary has committed himself to coaching individuals daily in increased understanding and application of the DNA message. He wants committed people who want the best relationship possible to practice taking control of their thinking and aligning it with God's thoughts (Phil 4:8, 9). He loves knowing that millions of people around the world are arm and arm in supporting each other through testimonies of life application and mutual commitment to great relationships. The world will know that Christ is real when they see our love for one another. He wants to join others in learning how to control core fears, how to create a safe place for love to flourish, how to take personal responsibility for all of our own emotions, words and actions, how to care for ourselves in order to have wisdom and energy to care for others, how to feel with others and communicate on the deepest levels possible, how to resolve conflicts with others as teams mates united in Christ and how to share our faith with others by living a genuine life in Christ. Let's do it together!
Visit our web site, www.smalleyonline.com and find out how you can join with millions of others around the world.

While on line, Churches can also join together with us in the Gary Smalley Relationship Network and gain access to the best Christian speakers in the world. Each month, various speakers will be live inside your church via satellite. We'll not only be training pastors in leadership skills, but in all aspects of ministry. We'll also include great training in the DNA message by numerous experts.

APPENDICES

Appendix A
Identify Your Core Fear

Appendix A

Identify Your Core Fear

1. IDENTIFY THE CONFLICT: Identify a recent conflict, argument, or negative situation with your spouse, friend, child, neighbor, coworker, or whomever that really pushed your buttons or upset you. Think about how you were feeling and how you wished the person would not say or do the things that upset you. You might have thought something like, "If only you would stop saying or doing _____, I would not be so upset".

2. IDENTIFY YOUR FEELINGS. How did this conflict or negative situation make you feel? Check all that applies—but star the most important feelings:

___ Unsure
___ Apathetic
___ Puzzled
___ Upset
___ Sullen
___ Sad
___ Hurt
___ Disappointed
___ Wearied
___ Torn up
___ Shamed
___ Uncomfortable
___ Confused
___ Worried
___ Disgusted
___ Resentful
___ Bitter
___ Fed up
___ Frustrated
___ Miserable
___ Guilty
___ Embarrassed
___ Frightened
___ Anxious
___ Horrified
___ Disturbed
___ Furious
___ Other: _____
___ Other: _____

3. IDENTIFY YOUR FEAR: How did this conflict make you feel about yourself? What did the conflict say about you and your feelings? Check all that apply, but star the most important feeling.

As a result of the conflict, (You fill in the example) I felt _____What That Feeling Sounds Like

Rejected——The other person doesn't want me or need me; I am not necessary in this relationship; I feel unwanted.

    Abandoned——The other person will ultimately leave me; I will be left alone to care for myself; the other person won't be committed to me for life.

    Disconnected——We will become emotionally detached or separated; I will feel cut off from the other person.

    Like a failure——I am not successful at being a husband/wife, friend, parent, coworker; I will not perform correctly; I will not live up to expectations; I am not good enough.

    Helpless——I cannot do anything to change the other person or my situation; I do not possess the power, resources, capacity, or ability to get what I want; I will feel controlled by the other person.

    Defective——Something is wrong with me; I'm the problem.

    Inadequate——I am not capable; I am incompetent.

    Inferior——Everyone else is better than I am; I am less valuable or important than others.

    Invalidated——Who I am, what I think, what I do, or how I feel is not valued.

    Unloved——The other person doesn't care about me; my relationship lacks warm attachment, admiration, enthusiasm, or devotion.

As a result of the conflict, I felt ____What That Feeling Sounds Like

    Dissatisfied——I will not experience satisfaction in the relationship; I will not feel joy or excitement about the relationship.

    Cheated——The other person will take advantage of me or will withhold something I need; I won't get what I want.

    Worthless——I am useless; I have no value to the other person.

    Unaccepted——I am never able to meet the other person's expectations; I am not good enough.

    Judged——I am always being unfairly judged; the other person forms faulty or negative opinions about me; I am always being evaluated; the other person does not approve of me.

    Humiliated——The relationship is extremely destructive to my self-respect or dignity.

Ignored——The other person will not pay attention to me; I feel neglected.

Insignificant——I am irrelevant in the relationship; the other person does not see me as an important part of our relationship.

Other _____

4. IDENTIFY YOUR REACTIONS: What do you do when you feel [insert the most important feeling from question #3]? How do you react when you feel that way? Identify your common verbal or physical reactions to deal with that feeling. Check all that applies but star the most important reactions:

Withdrawal——You avoid others or alienate yourself without resolution; you sulk or use the silent treatment.

Escalation——Your emotions spiral out of control; you argue, raise your voice, and fly into a rage.

Try harder——You try to do more to earn others love and care.

Negative Beliefs——You believe the other person is far worse than is really the case; you see the other person in a negative light or attribute negative motives to him or her.

Blaming——You place responsibility on others, not accepting fault; you're convinced the problem is the other persons fault.

Exaggeration——You make overstatements or enlarge your words beyond bounds or the truth.

Tantrums——You have fits of bad temper.

Denial——You refuse to admit the truth or reality.

Invalidation——You devalue the other person; you do not appreciate what he or she feels or thinks or does.

Defensiveness——Instead of listening, you defend yourself by providing an explanation.

Clinginess——You develop a strong emotional attachment or dependence on the other person.

Passive——You display negative emotions, resentment, and aggressive aggression in passive ways, such as procrastination and stubbornness.

Care taking——You become responsible for the other person by giving physical or emotional care and support to the point you are doing everything for the other person, who does nothing to care for him or herself.

Acting out ——You engage in negative behaviors, such as drug or alcohol abuse, extramarital affairs, excessive shopping or spending, or overeating.

Fix-it mode——You focus almost exclusively on what is needed to solve the problem.

Complaining——You express unhappiness or make accusations; you criticize, creating a list of the other person's faults.

Aggression ——You become verbally or physically aggressive, or possibly abusive.

Manipulation——You control the other person for your own advantage; you try to get him or her to do what you want.

Anger——You display strong feeling of displeasure or violent rage and uncontrolled emotions.

Catastrophize——You use dramatic, exaggerated expressions to depict that the relationship is in danger or that it has failed.

Numbing out——You become devoid of emotion, or you have no regard for others needs or troubles.

Humor——You use humor as a way of not dealing with the issue at hand.

Sarcasm——You use negative humor, hurtful words, belittling comments, cutting remarks, or demeaning statements.

Minimization ——You assert that the other person is overreacting to an issue; you intentionally underestimate, downplay, or soft pedal the issue.

Rationalization——You attempt to make your actions seem reasonable; you try to attribute your behavior to credible motives; you try to provide believable but untrue reasons for your conduct.

Indifference ——You are cold and show no concern.

Abdication——You give away responsibilities.

Self-Abandonment——You run yourself down; you neglect yourself.

5. Look at the items you starred in response to question 3. List the three or four main feelings. These are your core fears:

Core fear #1 _____

Core fear #2 _____

Core fear #3 _____

Remember that most core fears are related to two main primary fears:

1. The fear of being controlled (losing influence or power over others)

2. The fear of being disconnected (separation from people and being alone)

More men fear losing power or being controlled, and more women fear being disconnected from relationships with others.

Look at the items you starred in response to question 4. List your two main reactions when someone pushes your core fear button.

Reaction #1 _____

Reaction #2 _____

Your responses to these exercises should help you understand your part of the Fear Dance: your core fear button and your reaction. Remember that it's very common for your reactions to push the core fear button of the other person in the conflict. If the other person can figure out his or her core fears and reactions, you will see clearly the unique Fear Dance the two of you are doing. But even if the other person isn't able to be involved in the process of discovering his or her part of the Fear Dance, you can take steps to stop the dance.

APPENDIX B
DNA SMALL GROUP
COVENANT

DNA SMALL GROUP COVENANT

I commit myself to learning the core truths of the DNA message.

I will work out the truths in my everyday life.

I will accept you even though I may not always agree with you.

I agree to make myself available to the members of this group. I will be there when a group member is in need even if it is to just listen.

I promise to pray for you regularly.

I agree to become more open and share my true feelings, thoughts and relational struggles.

I will not share outside of the group what you say in the group. I agree to keep what is spoken in the group, in the group.

Small group will meet at _____
                           Date/time/place

_____ I acknowledge that showing up on time respects everyone in the group's time and effort. I pledge to make small group a priority in my family's schedule.

SIGNATURE: _____

DATE: _____

APPENDIX C
Memory Verses

I Will Pass All of My Thoughts Through the Following Grid
Finally, brothers, whatever is true, whatever is noble, whatever is right, whatever is pure, whatever is lovely, whatever is admirable—if anything is excellent or praiseworthy—think about such things. Whatever you have learned or received or heard from me, or seen in me—put it into practice. And the God of peace will be with you. Philippians 4:8, 9

Before I Speak, I Will Wait a Few Seconds to Change My Thoughts
My dear brothers, take note of this: Everyone should be quick to listen, slow to speak and slow to become angry... James 1:19

I Will Only Use Encouraging Words
Do not let any unwholesome talk come out of your mouths, but only what is helpful for building others up according to their needs, that it may benefit those who listen. Ephesians 4:29

I Will Thank God in Advance for JOY to Come From this Trial
Consider it pure joy, my brothers, whenever you face trials of many kinds, because you know that the testing of your faith develops perseverance. Perseverance must finish its work so that you may be mature and complete, not lacking anything. James 1:2-4

I Have Unlimited Power Through the Spirit of God
I pray that out of his glorious riches he may strengthen you with power through his Spirit in your inner being... Ephesians 3:16

I Can Control All of My Thoughts
We demolish arguments and every pretension that sets itself up against the knowledge of God, and we take captive every thought to make it obedient to Christ. II Corinthians 10:5

I Can Control My Tongue and Actions
We all stumble in many ways. If anyone is never at fault in what he says, he is a perfect man, able to keep his whole body in check. James 3:2

I Humble Myself By Admitting My Need for His Power
Or do you think Scripture says without reason that the spirit he caused to live in us envies intensely? But he gives us more grace. That is why Scripture says: "God opposes the proud but gives grace to the humble." James 4:5, 6